# American Legends: The Life of Nat King Cole

## By Charles River Editors

D1531489

# About Charles River Editors

**Charles River Editors** provides superior editing and original writing services across the digital publishing industry, with the expertise to create digital content for publishers across a vast range of subject matter. In addition to providing original digital content for third party publishers, we also republish civilization's greatest literary works, bringing them to new generations of readers via ebooks.

Sign up here to receive updates about free books as we publish them, and visit Our Kindle Author Page to browse today's free promotions and our most recently published Kindle titles.

# Introduction

**Nat King Cole (1919-1965)**

"If I could read it, I could play it." – Nat King Cole

A lot of ink has been spilled covering the lives of history's most influential figures, but how much of the forest is lost for the trees? In Charles River Editors' American Legends series, readers can get caught up to speed on the lives of America's most important men and women in the time it takes to finish a commute, while learning interesting facts long forgotten or never known.

Among the most recognizable and iconic vocal artists known to American society from the mid-twentieth to the twenty-first century, baritone Nat King Cole is indelible in the nation's consciousness for such hits as "Mona Lisa" and "Ramblin' Rose" as well as for his rendition of Mel Tormé's famous "Christmas Song," with the opening line known to millions of American households, "Chestnuts roasting on an open fire." Cole is almost synonymous with the Christmas holiday season. His entire career, following an early start as a first-rate pianist, includes a consistent string of similar hits, including: "Route 66," "Sweet Lorraine," "(I Love You) For Sentimental Reasons," "Nature Boy," "Too Young," "Answer Me," "Walkin' My Baby Back Home," "Straighten Up and Fly Right," "Lush Life," "Those Hazy Lazy Crazy Days of Summer," "People," "That Sunday That Summer," "Dear Lonely Hearts, "L-O-V-E," and "Unforgettable." His gentle baritone sound, elegant phrasing, and crystal-clear enunciation are unmistakable, and have remained as a beloved fixture in America's collective ear for well over half a century.

On the other hand, Cole, so well-known for just a fraction of his contribution to 20th century music, is one of the most anonymous and unexplored artists in the lexicon of great pop and jazz figures known to American and European audiences. Jazz devotees may know that, in his early years as a jazz pianist, he both studied with and influenced the greatest players, in his generation and those that followed. Those who regularly listen to the blues will find its distinct presence in his playing and can point to Cole's motion picture roles, one of which was the portrayal of the "Father of the Blues" himself, W.C. Handy. For those who love his singing, examples exist in multiple genres, and his image as a stage personality and host were smooth, unruffled, and elegant, putting him in good stead with others of his kind, such as Bing Crosby. And finally, despite his general bent toward tolerance and a non-violent response toward abuse, Cole's professional and personal stories are interwoven into the urge toward equal civil rights for African-Americans in the United States. Much like other famous singers, such as Marian Anderson, he fought ignorance and injustice, in part, by rising above it and providing a model for civilized behavior, both as a public figure and as an international musician. A professional performer who has continued to sell millions of records well past the date of his death, Nat King Cole also left a legacy, not only of an enormous body of recorded work, but in the career of his famous daughter, Natalie Cole. The United States feels nostalgia for Nat King Cole that it feels for few other artists, one that is easily triggered by the playing of any number of hits recorded over several decades. The strong strain of pianistic and vocal skills can be found in his "students" of the following generation, from pianist Oscar Peterson to singers George Benson and Johnny Mathis.

*American Legends: The Life of Nat King Cole* looks at the life and legacy of one of America's most famous musicians. Along with pictures of important people, places, and events, you will learn about Nat King Cole like never before, in no time at all.

American Legends: The Life of Nat King Cole

About Charles River Editors

Introduction

## Chapter 1: Early Years

"I'm a musician at heart, I know I'm not really a singer. I couldn't compete with real singers. But I sing because the public buys it." – Nat King Cole

Nathaniel Adams Coles was born in Montgomery, Alabama on March 17, 1919. The lack of a birth certificate, a common occurrence during that time in sections of the American South, caused some to place his birthdate in a two-year window, going as far back as 1917. Like many African-American families that migrated to the industrial centers of the Midwest and East in search of greater economic stability in the early twenties, Cole's family moved from the South to Chicago, Illinois when he was not yet five years of age.

Chicago was a great jazz center, and Cole, able to demonstrate significant musical talent by his teens, found himself living as a neighbor to Louis Armstrong and heard such artists as Earl "Fatha" Hines, the "father" of modern jazz piano, Art Tatum, the great keyboard virtuoso, Teddy Wilson, and clarinetist Jimmie Noone on a regular basis. Sneaking out to visit clubs was a regular feature of a childhood in such an environment, and in particular, he came under the spell of Hines, generally acknowledged as the most creative jazz pianist of his time, doing things no one else could do without supporting instruments. Many aspiring keyboardists were drawn to the South Chicago scene, and "every kid pianist in the Midwest copied Earl Hines."[1] However, no one really came close to joining his mentor on such a high level, except for Nat King Cole, and this occurred at a surprisingly young age for the precocious Cole. The mentoring was not official, but Cole didn't sneak out of the house, indiscriminately, to hear just anyone. He would "leave his apartment on Prairie Avenue, run several blocks through the dark, and stand outside the Grand Terrace Night Club…and listen to Earl's piano live from there."[2]

---

[1] Daniel Mark Epstein, Nat King Cole, New York Times – www.nytimes.com/books/first/epstein-cole.html
[2] Daniel Mark Epstein, Nat King Cole, New York Times

**Louis Armstrong**

**Hines**

Cole's father, Edwin James Coles, was a butcher by trade during the week, but aspired to preach on Sunday. He eventually succeeded in gaining a position as a Deacon of True Light Baptist and, later, at First Baptist. Cole's mother, Perlina, was involved with the music of the church choir as an organist. For her son to grow up in such an atmosphere of sacred music was all but given, and as so many African-American artists did, Cole received early training in sacred music, particularly on keyboards, from his mother. He recalls playing a good deal of music by the baroque composer, Johann Sebastian Bach, whose works are famous for developing both hands equally, but also reveling in the intense romanticism of Sergei Rachmaninov. Three brothers would also go on to sing or play professionally – Ike, Eddie, and Freddy. Two later brothers were named Isaac and Lionel, while Cole's sister, Evelyn, forsook the family's musical path to become a beautician.

**Freddy Cole in 2003**

By the age of 14, Cole had already established his first group, a 14-piece band called the "Royal Dukes." In a decidedly entrepreneurial spirit to gather such a number of players, he also put together a second band called "Rogues of Rhythm" and gave his attention to whichever one was getting the most work at the time. The size of these early ensembles may point to a later interest in more full orchestral accompaniments to his work, although his early career would be spent with trios and quartets, which was more apropos of the jazz genre with its intimate venues.

Cole's career at Wendell Phillips High School was not long-lived, and academic work did not mix well with his out-of-school musical exploits. For the young pianist, school was more about sports, which catered to his passionate love for baseball and, to a lesser degree, football. Later, he confessed to a love of almost all sports, the lone exception being horse racing. He once quipped, "The only sport I'm not interested in is horse racing, because I don't know the horses personally."[3] Cole was considered an above-average player on the gridiron, but he was even more gifted on the baseball diamond, at one point gaining the attention of professional scouts. Regardless, he dropped out of school before barely beginning his academic studies, and music,

---

[3] The Unforgettable Nat King Cole – www.natkingcole.com.50webs.com

not sports, took him away.

A young teenager bent on becoming a great jazz pianist could never have enjoyed this sort of experience in Montgomery, Alabama. "Jazz was bigger than any varsity sport on the South Side of Chicago in 1935. Any boy who could play five notes on a horn or pluck a fiddle string or bang a pot wanted to be in a band," stated Cole biographer Daniel Mark Epstein. By the age of fifteen, Cole was performing regularly with his brother Eddie, who had already toured with the Noble Sissle Band. Before his sixteenth birthday, Cole's name was already growing in the larger area of South Chicago, and he would soon find himself in league with many of the greats living there.

On one occasion, Cole unthinkably found himself in a battle of the bands as a late teen with Earl Hines himself. As a marketing ploy, those in charge of the jazz grapevine had begun to spread Cole's name around, until even the great Hines had to notice. Hines, heading up one of the country's best bands, had never heard of the kid from Montgomery, but he decided that it was a stroke of good marketing and agreed to participate. This put him in a bind, however. If he murdered the young man on the keyboard, audience sentiment would lean toward the challenge; yet, if he allowed Cole to outdo him in any way, his own position in the industry would be compromised. The bands alternated through the evening, throwing their best into the effort, and, in the end, Hines gave Cole his due as a fine talent, with no loss of prestige suffered. Epstein refers to the young Nat Cole, at that time and through Earl Hines' eyes, as "the kitten on the keys."[4] The elder artist continued as an object of the newcomer's admiration.

It was with his brother, Eddie, that Cole made his first professional recordings as pianist for Decca Records' "Sepia Series" with the "Solid Swingers" in 1936. These were referred to, at the time, as "race records,"[5] aimed solely at the African-American audience. In the same year, Eddie Cole's "Swingsters" was formed, and Nathaniel recorded two singles for Decca. In a short time, the ensemble came to be "much admired in jazz circles."[6]

Following the first Decca sessions, Cole, who had already developed a reputation as a fine jazz pianist, joined an all-black traveling revue entitled, "Shuffle Along," with its home base in Chicago. The music and lyrics had been penned by Noble Sissle and the great pianist, Eubie Blake, who would go on to a stellar performance and arranging career that lasted well into his 90s. The original "Shuffle Along" was premiered by the same composers in 1921 and set a mayoral race as its premise, from which came the great hit, "I'm Just Wild about Harry." The revived version of the 1930s show began with a six-week run in the city of Chicago before moving on to other points and, eventually, landing in California. Eddie left the tour before taking up temporary residence on the West Coast, but Nat stayed for the sake of being with his girlfriend, dancer Nadine Robinson. The two were married in 1937, once the tour ended. It is

---

[4] Daniel Mark Epstein, New York Times, Nat King Cole
[5] The Unforgettable Nat King Cole
[6] Encyclopedia of Alabama, Nat King Cole – www.encyclopediaofalabama.org/face/Article.jsp?id=h-1552

thought that Cole had not yet turned 18.

## Chapter 2: Early Music Career

**The Trio**

"For years the Trio did nothing but play for musicians and other hip people. We practically starved to death." – Nat King Cole

Creating a life without the support of the regular paycheck provided by the revue was extremely difficult for a young man in a new city, as well as not being recognized as a potential star, as he had been in Chicago. After much ground-breaking work, Cole began a steady regimen of playing in clubs, and he even led a big band for a short time, despite being only seventeen years of age. With his rapidly increasing skills at the keyboard, he was able to secure spots as a regular at the Century Club and for a forty-eight week run at the 331 Club, both in Los Angeles, despite being too young to legally play in either one. The Century Club was one of the hottest venues in Los Angeles for jazz devotees. Cole's playing caught hold there, and his reputation soared. Now, he was playing for people who could help him achieve his next steps. As one colleague noted, "All the musicians dug him. That cat could play."[7] Despite such acceptance, gaps in the work forced Cole to continue an itinerant lifestyle in the clubs; he was later quoted as saying, "I must have played every beer joint from San Diego to Bakersfield."[8]

Cole's piano virtuosity and harmonic sophistication came directly out of his experience with the playing of Earl "Fatha" Hines, who developed the "orchestral stride" and "trumpet" style of playing, fashioned to allow the piano sound to cut through in big venues, partly in thanks to his colleague, Louis Armstrong. Cole chose to follow this model consciously, especially after their meeting, but would, in time, find himself performing in more gentle venues, where his music was not intended to be mixed with the sounds of noisy audiences. For television and radio appearances, he was free to calibrate dynamics and touch as he pleased, and, thus, he was able to make use of the recording studio's subtleties, producing, at times, a less boisterous and flamboyant release of sound than Hines. Harmonically, he went in constant exploration, as Hines had done, and nothing was ever enough. The status quo of prevailing harmonic language would never last long with the two pianists on the circuit, and his playing grew increasingly impressionistic, at times resembling the harmonic language of the classical composer, Claude Debussy, from half a century before. Such a model suited him beautifully, as the moody intimacy fit perfectly with his sense of understated and elegant presentation, which, in turn, set the stage for his great command of vocal sentimentality.

During his time at the Century Club, Cole was approached in 1937 by the manager of the Swanee Inn, who sought his services in assembling a house band for the club. In bringing together the trio that would see him successfully through the rest of his keyboard career, Cole made excellent choices, both personally and musically, by hiring guitarist Oscar Moore and bassist Wesley Prince. The ensemble that resulted from this meeting was to become the "King Cole Swingsters," and, despite later personnel changes and tangents in their stylistic evolution, they remained one of the best small groups in the business. As the pianist, knowledgeable listeners could detect his origins at once, and the news around town was that Nathaniel "King" Cole "played a mean piano in the style of 'Fatha' Hines."[9] Count Basie himself spoke with nothing but superlatives, particularly in considering how quickly the trio came together – "Those cats used to read each other's minds – it was unbelievable."[10] Others seconded Basie's opinion,

[7] The Unforgettable Nat King Cole
[8] The Unforgettable Nat King Cole
[9] About Nat King Cole – www.natkingcole.com
[10] About Nat King Cole

as Cole developed with his two colleagues a sense of musical telepathy, something that all great groups possess.

An additional twist of fate allowed Cole to further develop as a pianist in terms of rhythm and harmony, freeing himself from the beat and filling in the subtle syncopations by which he had been inspired from watching and listening to Hines. The original idea was that the ensemble would be a quartet, with the standard drums included. However, drummer Lee Young failed to show up for the audition, and the group went "drummerless"[11] from that point on. To have a confining beat beneath him, one that could overpower him if he strayed from the pulse, would have stifled the looseness with which he played. As a result of Young's absence, the group developed a flexibility unknown to the more usual and rigid 4/4 bands. Such flexibility among instrumental ensembles would soon become a major innovation, playing with the same sense of elasticity that could be heard in the great singers, the ones who could sing between the beat for prolonged periods, without losing rhythmic stability. This became true, not only in instrumental circles, but for dancers and lead vocalists as well. Even for the audiences who came out to dance on a Saturday night, whatever their skill level, the rigid, almost European beat configurations of American dance forms gave way to a lithe and loose personal choreography provided for the American public by some of its best African-American artists. As for Cole the keyboard soloist, his early career as a "fleet-fingered, swinging, harmonically inventive jazz pianist"[12] had few rivals and many admirers.

By 1938, Cole had begun an extensive body of radio work, recording song transcriptions, discs not intended for commercial release, but specifically created for radio broadcasts with target audiences, usually on the 16-inch discs specific to radio stations of the time. His first radio appearances took place on NBC's "Blue Network," with subsequent broadcasts aired over the same network's "Swing Soiree." Such early experiences would propel Cole's presence on the air waves through the next few years, as he appeared at venues such as Old Gold, the Chesterfield Supper Club, and the Kraft Music Hall, under the supervision of host Bing Crosby. From these broadcasts came some of Cole's most elaborate examples of the blues, which he considered "an essential ingredient"[13] to almost any genre, such as the hit "Hit That Jive, Jack." The day on which the Swanee Inn's house band became formally known as the "King Cole Trio," it is reported that Cole's publicist put a tin foil crown on his head and "proclaimed him King."[14]

This would not be the first time that Cole was asked to perform while crowned as a less than subtle reference to the nursery rhyme and as a widely distributed promotional photo. The kinship of Cole's name to the famous children's verse, "Old King Cole," had been belabored from the very beginning of his musical pursuits, at times for official professional matters and, for others,

---

11 About Nat King Cole
12 Vincent Pelote, Review of "The Life and Mystique of Nat King Cole," Leslie Gourse, in NOTES Vol. 49 No. 3, March 1993.
13 NPR, Jazz Profiles
14 IMDb, Nat 'King' Cole Biography – www.imdb.com/name/nm0170713/bio

just in fun. Cole, never one to pass up a career advantage, seemed to accept the moniker with good humor.

   Over the next few months of 1939, Cole began to record with more high-profile artists, such as Lionel Hampton, and was invited to play many of the finest clubs in New York City and other metropolitan areas of the state, a few of which had previously been segregated by management policy and were just then opening up to popular presences, like Cole. The Trio spent several months in the city and never wanted for work or for valuable exposure. Through 1940, his first major examples of commercial offerings were recorded for Decca Records, and he established excellent associations with the great saxophonist Lester Young, an intimate associate of Billie Holiday, and bassist Red Callender. These venues, in which Cole made the most of his comfortable and easygoing style of presentation, opened doors in the film industry, while he continued to record with several smaller labels. In 1941, he recorded "That Ain't Right," which took off to a #1 ranking on the Billboard Harlem Hit Parade. The following single, "All for You," was recorded for the Excelsior label.

**Hampton**

**Young**

1942 saw the King Cole Trio take over as the house band at the 331 Club of Los Angeles, enjoying further associations with Lester Young and others. Cole, however, sensed that it was important to sing from time to time, if for no other reason than to break up the atmosphere of a set. While not taking himself seriously as a singer and having never given it any real thought, it became a new concept to Cole as well, to leave the keyboard and stand up front, like a real singer. He didn't think much of his baritone voice and didn't believe that it would elicit much attention over the long run. Yet, audiences and colleagues felt differently and took him quite seriously as a singer, constantly urging him to do more. His voice was described in a great variety of ways, as "rich, husky…[with] careful enunciation…warmth, intimacy and good humor

[in] his approach to singing."[15] As he did with his physical appearance and manner, he was officially reviewed as having a "smooth and well-articulated vocal style,"[16] an assessment that came as a complete surprise to him.

Cole continued to behave as a pianist who sang once in a while, still clinging to his spot at the bench, under the chandelier; however, he could not help but "notice that people started to request more vocal numbers, [and so] he obliged,"[17] In doing so, aided by impeccable timing, he became one of the first artists to record as a vocalist with Capitol Records, a corporation that would grow to gigantic and prestigious proportions in the industry. In fact, he would go on to record a breathtaking 700 songs for the label, becoming the first Capitol artist to rank #1 on the Billboard charts as well, with 150 charting singles in all. So successful and dominating in sales statistics was Cole that the corporation began referring to itself as "the house that Nat built."[18] And yet, he remained unimpressed with his own vocals, continuing to insist that his voice "is nothing to be proud of...I guess it's the hoarse breathy voice that some like."[19] Colleagues were mystified by such a self-description, given the extraordinary clarity for which he is so easily recognized and beloved. The only artist in the room who didn't see the wholesale move from jazz piano to front-stage singing star coming was Nat Cole himself.

[15] William Ruhlmann, All Music, Artist Biography, Nat King Cole – www.allmusic.com/artist/nat-king-cole-mn000317093/biography
[16] Bio.com, Nat King Cole Biography – www.biography.com/people/nat-king-cole-9253036#synopsis
[17] Star Pulse.com/Nat King Cole Biography – www.starpulse.com/Music/Cole,_Nat_King/Biography
[18] New World Encyclopedia, Nat King Cole – www.newworldencyclopedia.org/entry/Nat_King_Cole
[19] The Unforgettable Nat King Cole

**Nat in the late 1930s or early 1940s**

**Nat in 1947**

"I am famous because I am an African American jazz artist." – Nat King Cole

Once America joined the fighting in World War II, it became increasingly difficult to hold a band together, with members departing on short notice and replacements being increasingly hard to find. Prince, Cole's bassist, a player who had been carefully chosen and who knew the subtle nuances of the ensemble, would go with the draft. In addition, he began to sense that pure jazz was, at that time, drawing a diminished audience that would always harbor an elite minority, having always been the territory of the esoteric and intellectually oriented, at least in their own view. Cole began to realize that something with a broader appeal might lead to greater, more lucrative opportunities. He found himself exempt from the draft, and, although flat feet are cited as the cause by many, the official medical report named hypertension as the official reason. With other male stars heading to the European theater, Cole found roles in films such as *The Stork Club*, *Breakfast in Hollywood*, and *See My Lawyer*. Most of his film experience, from cameo to leading role, involved portraying musicians, sometimes appearing as himself. Being free from the draft and the ensemble requirements of collaborative jazz, all he needed was a piano and his own voice. Finally, he took the advice of almost everyone around him and reset his career to that of a singer.

In 1943, his first year with manager Carlos Castel, Cole's extensive solo piano work subsided, and he began to sing a regimen of fairly simplistic, but immediately nostalgic, hits for Capitol, beginning with a big success, "Straighten Up and Fly Right." Unfortunately for Cole, he had signed away the rights to the song some time back for a mere $50. Still, as the second #1 on the Harlem Hit Parade, the triumph inspired Capitol to sign him directly to a binding contract, courtesy of Johnny Mercer's invitation. The jaunty "Straighten Up and Fly Right" sold half a million copies, and although Cole didn't financially benefit from royalties, it served as ideal promotion for almost everything else he recorded for Capitol. His bank account prospered as well as his popularity ratings. As it turned out, the song was inspired by one of the sermons preached by Cole's father, in which a monkey "rode on the back of a treacherous buzzard,"[20] who was throwing off all of the other animals, and eating them. The monkey, however, wrapped his tail around the buzzard's neck, almost choking the bird, and survived; the message was to "get the monkey of one's back."[21] Unfortunately, the term "monkey" played into an unsavory racial insult that was used frequently in the war years.

---

[20] Encyclopedia of Alabama
[21] Encyclopedia of Alabama

**Mercer**

In the following year, "Straighten Up and Fly Right" and "Gee Baby, Ain't I Good for You" both topped the charts for several months. However, another recording of 1944 broke Cole's career wide open and guaranteed him a lasting legacy for anyone who celebrates Christmas, whether in religious or secular, commercial terms. The now iconic "Christmas Song," more commonly known as "Chestnuts Roasting on an Open Fire," was written by Mel Tormé (as a singer, endearingly known as 'The Velvet Fog') and Robert Wells, during a hot summer, with the admonition to "stay cool by thinking cool."[22] Despite many fine performances that offered well-recognized renditions of it, Cole's cover of the song would outdistance all others and continued to do so for more than half a century later, showing no signs of abating in popularity. Actually, "Christmas Song" was a gradual process, as Cole first recorded it with just piano over Capitol's objections. A second hit came in the same session with "(I Love You) For Sentimental Reasons."

---

[22] All Music, William Ruhlmann

**Tormé**

Not only was the vehicle of "Christmas Song" an enormously good choice for showcasing Cole's soothing singing style, but Capitol Records took the opportunity to get him off the piano bench at last and out in front of a full, string-heavy orchestra, with spectacular results. According to Cole, Capitol "felt that a big band (a general non-classical term that wind ensemble and full orchestra with strings) behind me would sell more records."[23]The studio was correct, and everything Cole recorded after "Chestnuts" surged in sales, regardless of whether accompanied by ensemble or lone keyboard.

1945 marked the first in which Billboard started to maintain the rankings charts. Cole and the trio were first in line with their recent hits and stayed at the original #1 spot for a period of 12 weeks. The declining fortunes of Cole's genre of choice, pure, abstract jazz, or "cool" jazz, as it went through various stages of experimental evolution, caused devotees to become increasingly interested in the appearance of bebop, where they could retain the fresh style of earlier jazz, without having to fathom the ever-changing and esoteric harmonies and rhythms. Cole continued to lean toward the 'easy-listening' pop numbers and received "numerous guest-star stints"[24] as a result.

---

[23] Nat King Cole, All About Jazz – www.musicians.allaboutjazz.com/natkingcole-piano
[24] All Music, William Ruhlmann

Perhaps the most important of them all was an invitation to appear on Bing Crosby's Kraft Music Hall radio series. Outside of racial considerations, Crosby and Cole were very much alike in terms of relaxed presence and as masters of the soothing style. Both men possessed warm, inviting instruments and enunciated clearly, without embellishment. Furthermore, they favored an almost identical style of repertoire. For an African-American artist attempting to break through the barriers of the business, Kraft Music Hall was a coup, especially since Cole would be personally invited to serve as Crosby's summer replacement as the host a year later. Cole also appeared in the film *See My Lawyer* in 1945, but it was the wave of show host invitations that were parlayed into such a degree of success. With the doors of Kraft open, virtually all of the great radio and television variety shows followed suit, including Ed Sullivan, Garry Moore, Milton Berle, and Perry Como. Despite his original prominence as an admired jazz pianist, it was as a gentle-voiced baritone, now standing up front, that Cole would be accepted into the highest venues of popular music. There were no more questions about his career direction. Still, in 1946, "Route 66" was recorded, a hit that would be covered later by such artists as Chuck Berry, Tom Petty, and the Rolling Stones. After reaching #3 on the charts and charting as a pop hit as well, "Route 66" has remained an R&B classic to the present day. Soon after, the second volume of the "King Cole Trio" was released, each volume containing two sets of 78 rpm recordings. "(I Love You) For Sentimental Reasons" reached the #1 spot on the pop single chart.

**Bing Crosby**

Nat King Cole's life took another major turn when he met the woman who would become his second wife, Maria Hawkins Ellington, at the Zanzibar Club in Los Angeles. Maria, widow of Tuskegee Airman Spurgeon Ellington, was not related to Duke Ellington, but had on one occasion performed with his band, was highly intelligent, talented, and had a clear head for career strategy in such an unpredictable industry. Possessing the personality with which to get what she wanted, or what she wanted for Cole, Maria had made no bones of the fact that he would be severely limited if he were to stay in the piano track, despite the greatest jazz keyboardists of the day, such as Art Tatum, hailing him as "one of the best pianists in the world."[25] Likewise, she knew at once that singing would not work out, either, unless Cole committed to it and stood out front, moving past the small ensemble format of the trio. Duke Niles, one of the "song-pluggers" in Cole's circle, seconded her opinion - "He couldn't just sit there and sing and become a big hit. He had to stand up and sing with strings."[26]Especially considering Cole's

---

[25] The Unforgettable Nat King Cole

understated stage style, sitting at a grand piano surrounded by television studio finery, all but swallowed him alive, but even in front, where he was suave and confident, his approach to singing was unchangeable – "Mine is a casual approach to a song; I lean heavily on the lyrics…tell a story with melody as background."[27] His lack of extensive range was, likely, a partial source of Cole's self-consciousness. It barely covered two octaves, but, in his defense, the repertoire didn't require any more than that, as it might in the operatic world. In fact, songwriters in general kept most of their material closer to the middle notes, to prevent the inevitable word distortions that take place at the extreme edges of the vocal range, a problem that is of less concern to operatic composers and singers.

[26] The Unforgettable Nat King Cole
[27] The Unforgettable Nat King Cole

# Nat and Maria

1946 was a controversial one, despite so much success. Leaving the jazz keyboard farther behind with each project, jazz lovers saw Cole's move to pop music as an utter betrayal and a waste of top-flight talent. The ensuing criticism leveled at Cole came from many sources, but most notably from publications such as *Downbeat* and *Metronome Magazines*, who accused him of abandoning the genre. With jazz's representative magazines stirring the pot, the outcry grew fierce for a question of musical career choices. Cole's response, despite the furor, was eminently practical, emotionally downplayed, and did not seem to suggest any great degree of nostalgia for his former days at the keyboard – "For years, we did nothing but play for musicians and other hip people…we practically starved to death."[28] He was quick to add that, "The people who know nothing about music are the ones that are always talking about it."[29]

Maria was especially adamant in not allowing Cole's thinking to be swayed by such criticism, and with little resistance, she took over his professional life almost entirely, very often to the trio's dismay. Her frank assessment of their relationship was, in the end, accurate – "What he needed, I had."[30] Her trajectory was to make the trio increasingly irrelevant over time, and no one seemed able to argue with her, least of all Cole. The well-educated Maria was thought by the trio to be "calculating…domineering, and snobbish,"[31] but she could not have cared less. Historically, Maria is thought to have had excellent vision for Cole, and she certainly protected him, not only from the outrage at his career change, but from his own self-doubts in making the decision to go ahead with it.

On some level, Cole still considered himself to be bogus goods when it came to singing and spoke as if every success meant that he had put something over on the public. More than once, he professed that, "I'm not really a singer. I couldn't compete with real singers. But I sing because the public buys it."[32] In more anonymous terms, however, he did not cease to play jazz altogether. Even though he had no need to appear in clubs or other jazz venues for financial reasons, he would pop up in establishments unexpectedly, presumably for the fun of it, and play under whimsical aliases such as Sam Schmaltz (a term that describes overly sentimentalized music) and Lord Calvert.

In 1948, Cole married Maria in Harlem's Abyssinian Baptist Church, with Adam Clayton Powell, Jr. presiding over the ceremony. Once divorced from Nadine, Cole plunged into his second marriage, although Maria's parents protested vehemently, believing that Cole was "too black." The couple, however, persisted, and together they had two daughters, Natalie and

---

[28] Performing Songwriter, Nat King Cole – www.performingsongwriter.com/natKing-cole/
[29] Am I Right, Nat King Cole – www.amiright.com/artists/natkingcole.html
[30] The New York Times, Maria Cole, Singer and Wife of Nat King Cole, Dies at 89 –
www.nytimes.com/2012/07/14/arts/music/maria-cole-jazz-singer-and-wife-of-nat-king-cole-dies-at-89.html?-r=0
[31] The Unforgettable Nat King Cole
[32] Am I Right, Nat King Cole

Caroline. Through difficult times, they would remain married for the rest of his life. Eventually, Cole had five children, three of them biological (daughters Natalie, Carol, and Timolin). Two were adopted, Carolyn and Kelly. In addition to the personal changes of 1948, Cole received his own radio show in the same year, sponsored by Wildroot Cream Oil. This was an impressive feat in the 1940s for any African-American artist, as corporations with high-profile products were skittish about sponsoring non-white media events, at the risk of offending Southern customers.

**Natalie Cole in 2013**

Cole's success in the latter part of the 1940s opened the door for a period of luxurious living, and, in seeking out a new home, he and Maria could not have made a more controversial choice than by moving to the Hancock Park area of Los Angeles. Granted, it was an enclave where many of the leading movie stars, business moguls, and politicians lived. In terms of tangible success, he was certainly the right type for the area, but Hancock Park was also a segregated community, complete with a localized legal document declaring that the neighborhood was "not for any person whose blood is not entirely that of the Caucasian race."[33] An addendum was added, indicating that the lone exception was for those working "in the capacity of servants." [34] Those of a more modern viewpoint must remember that such a document carried legal weight in the late 1940s, a decade and a half before the 1964 Civil Rights Act. Even honorably discharged African-American war heroes could not break the color barrier, so, for Cole, his bank account and résumé meant nothing in the all-white, affluent neighborhood of Hancock Park.

Natalie, Cole's now-famous daughter, was born in Hancock Park and describes her family life there as resembling being a member of the "Black Kennedys."[35] Memories of her father include his wish that his children should experience every sort of music possible, although when he found out that she was in love with Elvis and thought that her father should sing more rock, he remarked, "Mr. Cole does not Rock 'n' Roll."[36] She also refers to her many allergies. The one most hurtful to her father was her inability to be in the same room with the boxer dogs "that my father loved dearly."[37] Enumerating several of the neighborhood families in Hancock Park in her book, *Angel On My Shoulder*, she draws special attention to Governor Brown, the Shell Oil people, the Chandlers of the *Los Angeles Times*, the Vons Supermarket family, and others.

Upon first moving in, Cole received a letter from one of the residents, signed by others, that expressed the collective's unwillingness to allow "undesirables"[38] into the neighborhood. Natalie adds that the note specifically referred to not only African-Americans, but "Jews...people of ethnic persuasion."[39]Cole, in his best diplomatic English, responded in kind by informing the residents that if he were to meet an undesirable in the neighborhood, he would be the first to complain and would inform them at once. The slight tongue-in-cheek nature with which he handled the confrontation was not taken well, and the neighborhood followed by initiating legal action against him and his family, a case which was never successfully prosecuted. An attempt was made by several in the neighborhood to purchase Cole's house from him, but Cole and Maria staunchly refused. This not only met with "strong protests from white neighbors,"[40] but initiated a series of "questionable investigations by tax authorities."[41] It is unclear whether the neighborhood acted as a unanimous collective or whether a small group of specific members were involved. A few other of the immediate neighbors included Katherine Hepburn, who appears to be an unlikely candidate for committing racial exclusion, Mae West, and Howard Hughes. It was never made clear which of the families in Hancock Park took such overt action against the Cole family, but, at one point, Maria was driven to pen an impassioned letter to Eleanor Roosevelt herself as a plea for assistance.

[33] The Independent, The story of Nat King Cole and his racist neighbors – www.independent.co.uk/arts-entertainment/music/news/the-story-of-nat-king-cole-and-his-racist-neighbors-939316.html
[34] The Independent
[35] Natalie Cole, Angel On My Shoulder, written with Digby Diehl, 2000, Warner Books
[36] Natalie Cole
[37] Natalie Cole
[38] IMDb, Nat King Cole Biography
[39] Natalie Cole
[40] Encyclopedia of Alabama
[41] Encyclopedia of Alabama

Intimidation tactics reached a high pitch when Cole's dog was killed, after an unknown individual threw poisoned meat over the property wall. Racial insults were burned into Cole's front lawn, and, in general, the family experienced a considerable lack of safety in one of America's most affluent neighborhoods. Natalie's recollections also mention that, on one occasion, shots were fired through the front window and that a sign reading "Nigger Heaven" was pounded into the front lawn. The family persevered, however, and when it came time to leave Hancock Park some years later, Maria proudly sold the property to another African-American couple. In retrospect, Maria commented that, "Anyone who thought Nat was an Uncle Tom clearly did not know the man."[42] For all of his outer tranquility, he was capable of great stubbornness for the right reason.

The Uncle Tom stereotype was, indeed, precisely what many of Cole's critics thought of him, a star performer who was never able to find a comfortable place within the Civil Rights Movement, and one who would not stand up for his race. Although Hancock Park was neither the first nor last arena of racial conflict in Cole's life, he nevertheless "took the stance that he was an entertainer, not an activist,"[43] and he waged his own kind of war by being successful against the odds.

In 1949, Cole might well have asked why he was singing a song entitled "Mona Lisa." He was, in fact, heard to ask, "What kind of title is that for a song?"[44] In the beginning, he professed to not liking the number, but certainly did not criticize its success. With its customarily superior Nelson Riddle arrangement, "Mona Lisa," written by Ray Evans and Jay Livingston for the Paramount Pictures film *Captain Carey, U.S.A.*, sold three million copies and sat at #1 for a considerable length of time. The year also saw Cole on his first international tour, in which he played and sang at some of the top clubs in Europe, the Far East, and Latin America, coming home to appear at similarly prestigious venues in the United States and, in particular, at Las Vegas casinos. It soon became clear, however, that stardom, no matter how international, did not trump racial conditions, and he ended up suing a Pittsburgh hotel for refusing him a room, a hotel he probably could have bought. This was not an unfamiliar situation for America's best African-American artists, who would be hailed globally and appear by command performance for heads of state, only to return home where they could not sit at particular restaurants, book a room, or sing for an integrated audience. Cole gave a command performance for Queen Elizabeth, but was no king at home. Part of the problem, beside normal social conditions in America was, according to colleagues, that his easygoing manner permitted him to appear comfortable in any setting, also making him appear 'too equal' in white company. In hindsight, colleague Eartha Kitt observed that "Cole's sophisticated image, elegance, and interaction with white performers as equals was dangerous...too early."[45] Here he was, living in Hancock Park

---

[42] IMDb, Nat King Cole Biography
[43] Bio.com, Nat King Cole Biography
[44] Am I Right Nat King Cole
[45] New World Encyclopedia, Nat King Cole

with a box seat at Dodger Stadium, appearing in luxury suits, and singing in a world of grand pianos and chandeliers at white venues. Such success did not sit well with segments of white America, even while they bought his records. By joining figures like Paul Robeson and Marian Anderson as intellectually sophisticated performers, he presented a gracious and civilized image that could not be understood or accepted by citizens clinging to an old world less than a century after the Civil War.

## Chapter 4: The 1950s

"You've got to change with the public's taste." – Nat King Cole

As Cole entered the new decade, the transition from jazz pianist to pop singer was made complete. Beginning his career as "one of the most influential pianists and small-group leaders of the swing era,"[46] known throughout the business for his "compact, syncopated piano style with…clean spare melodic phrases,"[47] he went on to a parallel career, espousing these same qualities, simply and beautifully, without meaningless elaboration. By the mid-century, Cole was almost exclusively a singer, at least under his real name, although in serene televised settings, he often sat at the piano and accompanied himself. His "relaxed and humorous stage personality"[48] not only made for excellent hosting qualities, but was part of a persona one reviewer described as "a capable actor."[49] His original specialty, a form of 'cool' jazz, gave way to the same sort of vocal suave, with his "broad Southern accent and velvety voice,"[50] a far cry from his own description of "breathy and hoarse." His music, as before, was "easy on the ear,"[51] precisely the soothing manner that a nation, in the aftermath of wartime, craved in the golden age of crooners. The American audience was accepting him as the African-American counterpart to Bing Crosby, as far as comfort would allow.

In Cole's mind, the greatest hit of 1950 was the birth of daughter Natalie, nicknamed "Sweetie," who would grow up to follow in his footsteps as a much-admired singer. The musical hits in the early part of the decade included "Send for Me," "With You on My Mind," "When Rock & Roll Comes to Trinidad," and "Looking Back." "Too Young" came in 1951, becoming Cole's fourth #1 hit, eventually going gold, while the tune "Unforgettable" reached #12. Despite a ranking outside of the top ten, "Unforgettable" would go on to become one of Cole's most fondly remembered songs, made even more poignant by Natalie's re-issue decades later as a father/daughter duet. The 1951 announcement that the King Cole Trio was disbanding did not mean that they entirely ceased to perform together. Cole still took the instrumentalists along, but often incorporated them into the full orchestra. He offered up a retro jazz LP album in 1952, a

[46] Encyclopaedia Britannica, Nat King Cole – www.britannica.com/EBchecked/topic/125171/Nat_King-Cole
[47] Encyclopaedia Britannica
[48] Encyclopaedia Britannica
[49] Encyclopaedia Britannica
[50] Encyclopaedia Britannica
[51] All Music, William Ruhlmann

purely instrumental collection entitled "Penthouse Serenade." The album was oriented to slower tempi and reveled in harmonic exploration and dark, rich moods, rather than overt virtuosity. "Penthouse Serenade" never came close to appeasing the disenchanted jazz fans of a decade earlier, but, by this time, Cole had no need of seeking anyone's favor.

1953 started poorly for Cole's health, as he collapsed at a venue in New York City and was hospitalized for a week. The hospital listed his condition as critical and scheduled him for a stomach ulcer operation immediately, with "the most skilled surgeons in attendance."[52] Cole had planned a return to Los Angeles that week to prepare for an upcoming national tour, but doctors advised him that "a transcontinental flight might prove fatal."[53] Cole followed the recommendation of post-operative rest, and it did him much good.

Once on the mend, Cole found 1953 to be a good year for dramatic appearances, and he appeared in the film *Blue Gardenia*, earning a salary of approximately ten thousand. In that same year, he appeared in *Small Town Girl* and was seen in a television drama entitled *Song for a Banjo*. Never slowing down in his recording pace, he charted seven songs in 1953, with "Pretend" reaching #2. In the following year, five of his singles charted, and "Answer Me My Love" went gold. His 1954 album, *Nat King Cole Sings for Two in Love*, conducted and arranged by Nelson Riddle, reached the top ten and was used as a model by artists such as Frank Sinatra for later "theme" or "concept" albums.

In another historical milestone, 1954 became the year of what one biographer simply referred to as "The Show." Although Nat King Cole was not the first African-American to host his own television show (that honor goes to Hazel Scott, the first woman of color to do so as well), he was the first to do it on a major media outlet. While Scott's weekly jazz spot remained low-profile for a specific and narrower audience, and in contrast to her moving to Paris in order to escape McCarthyism, Cole went all the way with *The Nat King Cole Show* and worked hard to sustain it from week to week. The elaborate and sophisticated format consistently demonstrated "top production values"[54] and a first-rate orchestra with Nelson Riddle at the helm; with guest stars like Frank Sinatra, Sammy Davis Jr., Harry Belafonte, Count Basie, Peggy Lee, and Tony Bennett, the venture seemed incapable of failing. The show began as a fifteen-minute weekly program, but was soon expanded to a half-hour. Ratings more than merited its continuation, and many of the guest stars understood the social significance of the breakthrough, appearing either free or with drastically cut fees in order to help Cole succeed. In the end, however, despite the network's willingness to continue with the show, Cole himself pulled the plug, as not one corporate sponsor could be found to risk an association with a black artist in a hosting role, with a national television variety show bearing his name. After all the rhetorical camouflage was spent, it became clear that none of the major companies wanted to drive away any customers

[52] Flickr, Entertainment – www.flickr.com/photos/vielles_announce/3640513498/
[53] Flickr, Entertainment
[54] IMDb, Nat King Cole Biography

beneath the Mason-Dixon Line, which led Cole to observe, "I guess Madison Avenue is afraid of the dark."[55]

**A picture of *The Nat King Cole Show***

Cole, and many social progressives of both races, harbored great expectations for *The Nat King Cole Show*, as a way of normalizing the presence of African-Americans in white society and, in his words, as "a turning point so that Negroes may be featured regularly on television."[56] And, for a brief run of 64 episodes, it appeared to be serving that purpose. Nat King Cole was, "for

---

[55] IMDb, Nat King Cole Biography
[56] IMDb, Nat King Cole Biography

many white families…the first black man welcomed into their living rooms,"[57] and the creators of later offerings, from *The Jeffersons* and *The Bill Cosby Show* to specials featuring Belafonte, Mathis and the artists of Motown, can look back to Cole's pioneering effort in early television. Things moved more slowly in the deeper South, particularly in Mississippi, where television viewers complained of frequent "black-outs,"[58] in which the studio would experience "technical difficulties each time black faces were featured on NBC- or CBS-franchised programs."[59] Responses to such conditions, not only in the South, but nationwide, ranged from Dick Gregory's comment that "The only TV show that hires Negroes regularly is Saturday Night Boxing"[60] to the more subdued remark by Sidney Poitier that "I feel no joy in being a symbol."[61]

In the same year, Cole appeared on *The Ed Sullivan Show*, one of numerous such appearances. Cole was considered to be one of Sullivan's good friends, and the singer became a favorite guest on his show. As a means of being introduced to the pop arts world, *The Ed Sullivan Show* was the pinnacle among debut venues, but not all of the artists were new. Famed, veteran artists balanced the programming. With Cole, by that time a household name, his appearances may have, in some way, eased the sting of losing his show, but they also pressed home the point that he was still at the top of his profession. In one instance on the air, Sullivan presented Cole with a plaque, awarded to him from the Board of Managers of the Harlem Branch of the Young Men's Christian Association (YMCA). In the words of Sullivan, the award was offered because "He is a king who has not lost the common touch."[62]

---

[57] The Unforgettable King Cole
[58] Sharon Monteith, Review of "Watching Jim Crow: The Struggles Over Mississippi T, 1955-1969", Steven D. Classen, *The Journal of American History*, Vol. 92 No. 1 (Jun., 2005), p. 297
[59] Sharon Monteith, Watching Jim Crow
[60] Fred Macdonald, Review by A. Robert Lee, "Blacks and White TV: Afro-Americans in Television since 1948", in *Journal of American Studies*, Vol. 19 No. 2 (Aug., 1985), p. 277
[61] Fred Macdonald, *Journal of American Studies*
[62] The Official Ed Sullivan Site, Quotes – www.ed.sullivan.com/ed-sullivan-show-quotes

**Ed Sullivan**

Cole continued his winning ways in 1955 with 8 charting songs within the Top Ten, including "Darling Je Vous Aime Beaucoup," "A Blossom Fell," "If I May," and continued success with Tormé's and Wells' "Christmas Song." "Darling Je Vous Aime Beaucoup," a song written in 1935 by Anna Sosenko, reached #7. The year 1955 also marked the occasion in which the King Cole Trio was finally disbanded after becoming little more than "window dressing"[63] to his more elaborate venues. With the addition of "Non Dimenticar," Cole could barely lose, and a flop from him was almost unheard of. His recordings were "practically legal tender,"[64] so reliable that

[63] The Unforgettable Nat King Cole
[64] Daily News, Nat King Cole Documentary Showcases Singer's Struggle with Racism, 1940s, 1950s, Los Angeles

he could choose his projects at will without fear of rejection within the studio structure.

In 1956, however, Cole learned again that no amount of success was a buffer against overt racism. At the height of his success, Cole was attacked in a live performance by members of a white supremacy group called the White Citizens Council, injuring his back on the stage of the Birmingham Municipal Auditorium. The group that would later come to be known as the Conservative Citizens Council was purportedly attempting to kidnap Cole. Their purpose behind the intended abduction was not clear, but whatever the case, during the third song of the evening, a romantic ballad named "Little Girl," four men ran down the aisle and stormed the stage to the screams of "Let's go get that coon."[65] They reached the stage unimpeded, and Cole was grabbed and wrestled to the floor. A group of undercover police rushed forward to assist him, but, unfortunately, uniformed police officers were not aware of the plainclothesmen and assumed they were attackers instead, detaining them while the attack on Cole continued. Falling to the floor, he was hit in the face by the microphone and suffered injuries to his back.

The back-up band for the evening was the Ted Heath Orchestra. As a British band, it seemed to make sense that they strike up "God Save the Queen," a common habit for such commotions in the UK, but it had little or no effect on a Southern American mob. Once a semblance of order was restored, Cole returned to the stage and addressed the audience – "I just came here to entertain you. I thought that was what you wanted. I was born here. These folks have hurt my back. I cannot continue, because I have to go for a doctor."[66] In a state of shock at being "denied the most basic civil rights in his own country"[67] after such widespread acceptance throughout the globe, perhaps Cole was somewhat naïve in the moment, thinking that he had been given a free pass, or perhaps it was that the same level of vitriol was not present in his personal nature. Nevertheless, he never returned to the South for live performances, even in his home town. As a symbol, however imprecise, Cole addressed the Republican Party Convention that year, as he would the Democratic Convention two years later.

Author Bernard Powers speaks of Cole's attack in Birmingham at length, analyzing it in the broader view of the Civil Rights Movement and the state of the Southern "mind" at the time. In Powers' view, the more overtly racist South (as opposed to the more subtly racist North) was beset by two primary fears, the first being "aggressive civil rights activism."[68] The other was, plain and simple, a fear of "rock 'n' roll music associated with the Black culture...threaten[ing] to undermine white values."[69] Unfortunately for Cole, in that time and in that location, he

---

– www.nydailynews.com/entertainment/tv/nat-king-cole-doc-showcases-singer-racist-neighbors-article-1.1797099

[65] Brian Ward, "Civil Right and Rock and Roll: Revisiting Nat King Cole Attack of 1956," OAH Magazine of History, Vol. 24, No. 2, April, 2010

[66] OAH Magazine of History

[67] Vincent Pelote

[68] Bernard E. Powers, Jr. College of Charleston, Review of "Race and Class in the American South," Melvyn Stokes, Rick Halpern, in The Journal of American History, Vol. 82 No. 2, (Sept., 1955), p. 776

[69] Bernard E. Powers, Jr., p. 776

"embodied both"[70] with the added insult of appearing as an elite white, making him an obvious and easy target.

At the end of 1956, Cole made one more trip down memory lane and released a jazz album entitled *After Midnight*. In this album, he proved beyond any doubt that he could sing vocal improvisations and not "just regular crooning."[71] What had been heard before in his piano skills was now, for the first time, apparent in his vocal ability as well. Soon after, he made appearances in the films *China Gate*, starring Gene Barry and Angie Dickinson, and *Istanbul*, starring Errol Flynn. Of note is that Cole was paid only five thousand dollars for appearing in *China Gate* and yet was paid seventy-five thousand for singing "Three Coins in a Fountain" for the opening credits. Such was the magnitude of his status as a singer over that of an actor.

If Cole was ever to toy with the genre of rock music, despite his protestations to daughter Natalie, the closest he ever came was in 1957, with "Send for Me," which was recorded with a trio, three guitars, "honking sax and gritty vocals."[72] Although he never went that way again, "Send for Me" topped the Billboard charts for two weeks. What might have transpired had he made the experiment a more serious one is entirely open to speculation, but he never risked losing an enormous listenership in a second genre change, especially in his late thirties. The next hit for 1957 was a return to the familiar, with a ballad album entitled *Love is the Thing*, which sat at #1 for eight weeks and eventually went platinum.

The largest cinematic project in which Cole ever participated came in 1958, when he was engaged to play the role of W.C. Handy in a film on the great blues musician's life. Cole guest-starred along with luminaries such as Eartha Kitt, Cab Calloway, Pearl Bailey, Ella Fitzgerald, Mahalia Jackson, and Ruby Dee. Of all his film ventures, it was the only starring role Cole ever played, and he played it with much success. W.C. Handy himself, a consultant on the film, died just a few days before the film's release. Although "Looking Back" charted in the same year, Cole's popularity began to fade in the latter part of the decade, only to resurge unexpectedly in the early 1960s. A new generation of crooners, like Johnny Mathis and Harry Belafonte, was gaining prominence, and no style that remains stagnant endures for long in the music business. In addition, "the rise of rock music diminished his success"[73] and, in the coming years, would threaten almost all other genres with being bound to either nostalgic or specialty markets, except for the very top artists.

In historical terms, it is unusual for an artist of a rapidly evolving genre to rebound from near obsolescence in just two or three short years. More often than not, they must wait for a future generation to rediscover and exalt them as retro gold. Nat King Cole was never relegated to obsolescence in the first place, and he never lost his audience. Likewise, the next generation

---

[70] Bernard E. Powers
[71] Encyclopedia of Alabama
[72] About Nat King Cole – www.natkingcole.com
[73] All Music, William Ruhlmann

never needed to rediscover him, as he was ingrained into the Christmas culture of all who celebrated it. New fans knew precisely who he was from their own childhoods.

In the last months of the 1950s, Cole worked in the studio with Louis Armstrong, Ella Fitzgerald, and Nelson Riddle. He befriended Frank Sinatra as well, an artist who feared no one, including racial extremists who threatened him or his friends. Sinatra was unflinching in his support of Cole's rocky times.

## Chapter 5: Final Years

"People don't slip. Time catches up with them." – Nat King Cole

Cole's final acting role was filmed in *Night of the Quarter Moon* and, after a spring tour of Latin America, he adopted son Nat Kelly. Cole performed for the inauguration of John F. Kennedy in 1960 and, in the same year, put together a Broadway revue, eventually creating an album from its songs entitled *Wild is Love*. The album reached the top ten charts for the first time in over three years. Tasting the old success once again, Cole attempted another follow-up stage show corresponding with the album entitled, "I'm With You," but the show enjoyed far less success, opening in Denver and closing by the time it reached Detroit, never to open in New York as he had hoped. A persistent Cole tried yet again to assemble a successful stage enterprise from the debris of the last ones, entitled "Sights and Sounds: The Merry World of Nat King Cole," including a host of singers and dancers under the name of the "Merry Young Souls." "Sights and Sounds" toured with far greater success than the previous effort for the next three years.

Audiences would, much later, fall in love with the father/daughter duet of "Unforgettable," accomplished through advances in sound technology, but Natalie's enchanting recreation was not the first occasion on which the two sang together. 1961 marks the year in which Cole sang a duet in the flesh with his daughter, introducing her to his public at the age of six and again at 12.

Soon after, "Ramblin' Rose" was released, written by Joel and Noel Sherman. The 1962 hit marked the first time in four years that a Cole single reached the top ten. The "country-tinged"[74] classic, and the album of the same name, broke all the records Cole had already set and, over time, went platinum, spending a stretch at #1 on the Adult Contemporary, #2 for R&B, and #2 for pop songs. It even went to #1 in Australia for several weeks. Cole's final charting single came out in the summer of 1963, "Those Hazy Lazy Crazy Days of Summer," with its jaunty lilt and nostalgic tinges of old honky-tonk days. Producers hoped to lure Cole back into the jazz world for a 1964 instrumental album, including tracks on which he would play the organ, another talent almost never heard by his new audience. Unfortunately, it was never made.

In December 1964, Nat King Cole was admitted to St. Johns Hospital in Santa Monica and

---

[74] All Music, William Ruhlmann

diagnosed with a case of lung cancer. The state of its advancement was not clearly determined at first, but, regardless, the regimen of treatment was an intensive one. At his first examination, in fact, his prognosis was thought to be a fairly good one, and he continued to work wherever and whenever possible. He was even able to appear in the film *Cat Ballou* with Jane Fonda and Lee Marvin and to record one more album for Capitol Records, *L-O-V-E*. His last two ballad titles ring poignantly and, perhaps, prophetically for the time - "I Don't Want to Hurt Anymore" and "I Don't Want to See Tomorrow."

**Nat in 1964**

During the month of December, Cole underwent a series of cobalt and radiation procedures, and, despite the blunt nature of such treatment of lung cancer in that decade, he rallied for a time. Only days before his death, he was making public appearances, looking reasonably well, and telling his followers, "I am feeling better than ever. I think I've finally got this cancer licked."[75] In January, he underwent an operation to remove his left lung, but, on February 15, 1965, he died

---

[75] New World Encyclopedia, Nat King Cole

of cancer in the other lung and other areas where the disease had spread.

Cole had been a heavy smoker for many years, and those who knew him practically could not remember a time where he was seen without a cigarette in his hand. His brand was Kool Menthols, and he professed a belief that it was the cigarettes that gave him a low, rich sound, whereas, in most cases, smoking dries the vocal timbre, limits functionality on top notes, and creates a growl in the approximate half-step note it creates on the lower end. For the sensation of singing, the vocal experience resembles waking up groggy and congested, creating the impression of added power in the low notes. Cole smoked an average of three packs a day and, on some level, may have felt compelled to do so as a way of "generat[ing] revenue from television advertisements promoting tobacco."[76]

Maria was present during these final days, but the two were not together. Cole had been involved in a series of affairs throughout their marriage, most notably with actress Gunilla Hutton of *Hee Haw* fame, and relations between Nat and Maria were often strained.

**Hutton**

---

[76] Find A Grave, Nat King Cole – www.findagrave.com/cqi-bin/fg.cgi?page=gr&GRid=1336

Cole, who died at the age of 45, was buried in the Freedom Mausoleum of Forest Lawn in Glendale, California. Among the stars and other celebrity admirers who attended his funeral were Robert F. Kennedy, Rosemary Clooney, Frank Sinatra, Jack Benny, Governor Pat Brown, Count Basie, Thomas Riddle, Billy May, David Cavanaugh, Steve Allen, Jimmy Durante, and Leonard Feather.[77] The Assembly of the State of California issued an announcement immediately afterward that read, "His voice, his touch on the piano, these will be missed, but the loss of Nat King Cole the man is the greatest."[78]

Following his death, Cole's work failed to draw the attention of a new audience, partly because he was already in the American musical DNA. There was no corner of American popular arts in which he was not known. His body of recordings did not, therefore, foster any new movements or present a daring new musical paradigm to the public. No revivals of his vocal work were necessary, as he had never disappeared from the scene.

That said, Cole's jazz recordings were all but forgotten for a time, except by those who cherished the early phases of his career. Where he had explored daring harmonies at the keyboard, he used his voice to soothe listeners with the traditional sound and phrasing. While he did not gather a new listenership, the one he amassed during his lifetime was galvanized into one of the most loyal fan bases in the history of music, classical or non-classical. Compilations and reissues were omnipresent, as every small and mid-level record company rushed in to make a quick buck before Cole's magic grew cold. American culture could not think of celebrating the Christmas season without the presence of his voice in Mel Tormé's masterpiece pouring from speakers in every store, from outdoor exhibits onto the streets, and in every televised celebration. Unfortunately, in Europe, the statute of limitations for recordings was considerably shorter than in the U.S., a period of fifty years. That has resulted in "a spate of low-quality re-issues."[79]

While some might think of Cole as too much of a traditionalist who never moved forward after the fading of his era, others view his insistence on simple, plainly beautiful singing, without elaborating to the point of losing recognition of the song itself, as a demonstration of his integrity. Jay Cocks of *TIME Magazine* wrote of Cole, "He wasn't corrupted by the mainstream. He used jazz to enrich and renew it, and left behind a lasting legacy. Very much like a king."[80] The artist who garnered twenty-eight gold record awards and, over time, more than one platinum was hailed by his audience and colleagues as the greatest of his era in several respects. The force of his warm personality and treatment of others was not forgotten by his industry or by his friends. In the year of Cole's death, Sammy Davis, Jr. performed a moving musical tribute to Cole on his NBC Television Special, "The Best on Record."

---

[77] New York Public Library, Nat King Cole Papers, Schomburg Center for Research in Black Culture – www.nypl.org/sites/default/filed/archivalcollections/pdf/cole_nat_K.pdf
[78] Historical News, *The Journal of Negro History*, Vol. 50 No. 2 (April, 1965), p. 145
[79] All Music, William Ruhlmann
[80] The Unforgettable Nat King Cole

One of three biographies that are generally accepted as the most important accounts of Cole's life and career was published in 1971 by his wife, Maria –*Nat King Cole: An Intimate Biography*. Considered to be well-written and thankfully uncluttered, economical, and clear for having been written by a spouse, Maria shed light on Cole, the man and the artist, from perspectives that no one else could have held, although it is noted that some "unpleasant details"[81] were omitted from the manuscript.

In 1974, Cole's recording of "Christmas Song" received a National Academy of Recording Arts & Sciences Hall of Fame Award, and in 1989, he received, posthumously, a Lifetime Achievement Grammy Award before being inducted into the Alabama Jazz Hall of Fame in the following year, under the category of "Lifework."

Natalie Cole created a sensation through the 1991 melding of her voice with that of her father's. Reaching across time, she took Cole's hit track of "Unforgettable" and intertwined it with her own, creating a masterful and poignant duet between the generations without ever stepping on what it was that made her father's solo rendition so penetrating. Skillfully and tastefully formatted, the duet across generations began by having the voices alternate lines before growing closer together in the final verses, uniting both the vocal and the father-daughter intimacy. Natalie carried on the family tradition in a manner that would have made her father proud by investing the same heart connection into her own work that her father had always invested in his and by putting their vocal skills together, which created an enormous posthumous hit, taking "Unforgettable" even farther than it had ever been in audience appreciation. The song won seven Grammys in the 1992 Awards Ceremony.

A second important biography on Cole's life and work came out in 1991, this time authored by Leslie Gourse, an experienced researcher on the subject. In her book, *Unforgettable: The Life and Mystique of Nat King Cole*, she delved into a "more thorough analysis of his music,"[82] where Maria had concentrated more on the personal uniqueness of the man and his music.

In the early 1990s, children Casey and Tamolin established a foundation in the state of Florida, dedicated to furnishing "materials for music education to state public school,"[83] a cause that their father would most certainly have applauded. In the year of 1993, Cole was inducted into the Big Band Hall of Fame, but two years later, he would lose his son Kelly to the AIDS virus. Induction into the Downbeat Jazz Hall of Fame came in 1997, and the third great biography, that of Daniel Mark Epstein, was published in 1999, a happy balancing of the first two, having the benefit of studying both works as sources.

A commemorative stamp was issued by the Federal Post Office in 1994, which overtly omits any image of Cole smoking. His name and likeness would be invoked frequently in the fight

[81] Daniel Mark Epstein, Nat King Cole: Review by Phillip D. Atteberry – www.pitt.edu/-satteberry/jazz/articles/natcole.htm
[82] Encyclopedia of Alabama

against smoking over the years, particularly in anti-smoking campaigns directed at the young.

At the advent of the 21st century, Cole was remembered as fondly as he had ever been, being inducted into the Rock & Roll Hall of Fame in 2000 under the generally unfamiliar category of "Early Influence." In the awards ceremony that year, Ray Charles served as Cole's presenter. One of the most complete compilations of Cole's music came out in 2005 from Capitol Records and EMI, entitled *The World of Nat King Cole*, and 2007 saw his induction into the Hit Parade Hall of Fame. Maria, who had been married to Cole for seventeen years, died in Boca Raton, Florida, at the age of eighty-nine in 2012.

Nat King Cole was awarded two stars on the Hollywood Walk of Fame, one for his television work and the other for his recordings. Considering his one hundred pop single hits, with over two dozen charting albums over the space of twenty years, Cole stands (statistically) only behind Frank Sinatra as the most successful artist of his generation. Particularly uncanny is that well over half a century following his death, he still manages to sell around one million recordings per year, after selling twenty-eight million in his lifetime. Among traditional genres, he broke ground for many other artists, offering some of the first jazz concerts ever given with pre-existing Philharmonic orchestras, and, although Daniel Mark Epstein's writings on Cole are considered too academic by some, the author more fully explains the depths to which the artist could go, on the keyboard, with the voice, or through social turmoil. Epstein also points out the vastness of Cole's influence to the artists who came after him. At the bottom of it all, however, was a man who took the simple approach, never turning down a successful enterprise or complaining of inauthenticity in his profession, but proceeding through his professional and personal life as "a gentle, tolerant and gracious human being."[84] When all was said and done, his life's goal, as it finally worked itself out, was equally simple – "All I want to do is sing and make people happy."[85]

It is uncommon for an artist to make a severe shift in the middle of their career, and those who attempt it are usually consigned to oblivion in terms of wide audience appeal. That Cole was eminently successful in the jazz keyboard world before even entertaining the thought of singing is noteworthy, and for one to take his own vocal gifts with such little seriousness rarely generates a recognizable career. Cole, however, despite his self-deprecating views on his own voice, succeeded brilliantly on both fronts, choosing the larger vocal standard market because he enjoyed it and because he recognized its larger career potential. He is only less known as a pianist because the pure jazz market was, and always has been, a smaller, more specialized professional arena. Cole was, then, the professional artist who succeeded at everything he attempted, whether he intended to follow through with it or not, and he accomplished the transition with an enormous degree of support from his family and his primary studio, Capitol Records.

---

[84] All About Jazz, Nat King Cole – www.,usicians.allaboutjazz.com/natkingcole-piano
[85] IMDb, Nat King Cole Biography

Nat King Cole was not interested in experimenting in all directions with vocal styles. Whether he enjoyed rock music, for example, is unknown, but he was vehement in staying away from the genre as a performer. He sang and played without artificial flash, remaining dignified and authentic to the text. Where he had once explored the depths of modern harmony at the piano, joining some of the most esoteric and virtuosic jazz pianists of the time, he stuck to the standards with his singing and never moved from an era-specific, post-war sentimentality that seemed to be just what the country needed. Unchallenged as the finest jazz pianist in Los Angeles, that is, until the arrival of Art Tatum, he almost gladly turned over the title to the newcomer and grew into one of the most iconic vocal and visual images of any musical genre in any era. And, in terms of one seasonal song, he ensured that he would never have to reintroduce himself to another generation again, so long as Americans still celebrated Christmas.

## Bibliography

About Nat King Cole – www.natkingcole.com

All Music, William Ruhlmann, Artist Biography, Nat King Cole – www.allmusic.com/artit/nat-king-cole-m000317093/biography

Am I Right, Nat King Cole – www.amiright.com/artists/natkingcole.html

Bio.Com, Nat King Cole Biography – www.biography.com/people/nat-king-cole-9253036#synopsis

Cole, Natalie, *Angel on My Shoulder*, written with Digby Diehl, 2000, Warner Books

DailyNews, Nat King Cole Documentary Showcases Singer's Struggle with Racism in 1940s, 1950s, Los Angeles – www.dailynews.com/entertainment/tv/nat-king-cole-dec-showcases-singer-racist-neighbors-article-1.1797099

Encyclopaedia Britannica, Nat King Cole – www.britannica.com/EBchecked/topic/125171/Nat-King-Cole

Encyclopedia of Alabama, Nat King Cole – www.encyclopediaofalabama.org/face/Article.jsp?id=h-1552

Epstein, Daniel Mark, New York Times, Nat King Cole – www.nytimes.com/books/first/epstein-cole.html

Find A Grave, Nat King Cole – www.findagrave.com/cqi-bin/fq.cqi?page=gr&GRid=1336

Historical News, *Journal of Negro History*, Vol. 50 No. 2 (April, 1965), p. 145

IMDb Nat "King" Cole Biography – www.imdb.com/name/nm0170713/bio

Monteith, Sharon, Review of "Watching Jim Crow: The Struggles Over Mississippi TV, 1955 – 1969, Steven D. Classen, *The Journal of American History*, Vol. 92 No. 1 (Jun., 2005). P. 297

Nat King Cole, All About Jazz – www.musicians.allaboutjazz.com/natkingcole-piano

Nat King Cole Biography, Encyclopedia of World Biography – www.notablebioggrraphies.com/ch-co/Cole-Nat-King.html

Nat King Cole, Daniel Mark Epstein, Review, Phillip D. Atteberry – www.pitt.edu/-atteberry/jazz/articles/natcole.htm

New World Encyclopedia, Nat King Cole – www.newworldencyclopedia.org/entry/Nat_King_Cole

New York Public Library, Nat King Cole Papers, Schomburg Center for Research in Black Culture –www.nypl.org/sites/default/filed/archivalcollections/pdf/cole/_nat__k.pdf

NPR, Jazz Profiles, Nat King Cole: The Pianist – www.npr.org/2008/02/06/18715138/nat-king-cole-the-pianist

Performing Songwriter, Nat King Cole – www.performingsongwriter.com/nat-king-cole/

Powers, Bernard E., Jr., College of Charleston, Review of "Race and Class in the American South", Melvyn Stokes, Rick Halpern, in the *Journal of American History*, Vol. 82 No. 2 (Sep., 1955), p. 776

Rock & Roll Hall of Fame, Nat "King" Cole Timeline –www.rockhall.com/story-of-rock/timelines/nat-king-cole/basic/

Star Pulse.com, Nat King Cole Biography – www.starpulse.com/Music/Cole,_Nat_King/Biography/

The Independent, The Story of Nat King Cole and His Racist Neighbors – www.independent.co.uk/art-entertainment/music/news/the-story-of-nat-king-cole-and-his--racist-neighbors-9391316.html

The New York Times, Maria Cole, Singer and Wife of Nat King Cole, Dies at 89 – www.nytimes.com/2012/07/14/arts/music/maria-cole-jazz-singer-and-wife-of-nat-dies-at-89.html?_r=0

The Official Ed Sullivan Site, Quotes – www.edsullilvan.com/ed-sullivan-show-quotes

The Unforgettable Nat King Cole – www.natkingcole.com.50webs.com/biography

Vincent Pelote, Review of "The Life and Mystique of Nat King Cole" by Leslie Gourse, in *NOTES*, Vol. 49 No. 3, March, 1993

Ward, Brian, "Civil Rights and Rock and Roll: Revisiting the Nat King Cole Attack of 1956, *OAH Magazine of History,* Vol. 24, No. 2, April, 2010

Cuyahoga Valley Christian Academy
4637 Wyoga Lake Rd.
Cuyahoga Falls, Ohio 44224
330-929-0575

31845457R10028

Made in the USA
San Bernardino, CA
21 March 2016